READING POWER

EXTREME SPORTS™

Snowboarding

CHECK IT OUT!

Kristin Eck

The Rosen Publishing Group's
PowerKids Press™
New York

SAFETY GEAR, INCLUDING HELMETS, SHOULD BE WORN WHILE SNOWBOARDING. DO NOT ATTEMPT TRICKS WITHOUT PROPER GEAR, INSTRUCTION, AND SUPERVISION.

For Mike

Published in 2001 by The Rosen Publishing Group, Inc.
29 East 21st Street, New York, NY 10010

First Edition

Book Design: Michael de Guzman
Layout: Felicity Erwin

Photo Credits: p. 5 © International Stock/Peter Kinninger; p. 7 © International Stock/Kirk Anderson; p. 9 © Thaddeus Harden; pp. 11, 13, 21 © Nathan Bilow/Allsport U.S.; pp. 15, 19 © Agence Vandystadt; p. 17 © International Stock/Eric Sanford.

Eck, Kristin.
    Snowboarding : check it out! / Kristin Eck.
       p. cm.— (Reading power) (Extreme sports)
    Includes bibliographical references and index.
    Summary: This book describes snowboarding, including information on the equipment for the sport, the skills for Alpine and freestyle snowboarding, and the safety precautions.
    ISBN 0-8239-5694-6
    1. Snowboarding—Juvenile literature. [1. Snowboarding] I. Title. II-III. Series.
2000
796.9—dc21

Manufactured in the United States of America

Contents

1 On the Snow 4

2 The Gear 6

3 Alpine 12

4 Freestyle 14

5 Glossary 22

6 Books and Web Sites 23

7 Index/Word Count 24

8 Note 24

Snowboarding is fun. You ride a board on the snow.

A snowboarder needs a helmet and goggles. Snowboarders need warm clothes, too.

7

There are lots of different
kinds of snowboards. They
are different colors. They
are different sizes.

A snowboard has bindings. Bindings keep your boots on the board.

11

Alpine is one kind of snowboarding. You go fast down a hill.

Freestyle is another kind of snowboarding. You go high in the air. You do different tricks.

15

There are lots of snowboarding tricks. One trick is called air to fakie. You turn in the air.

People watch snowboarders do tricks. Snowboarders do tricks in the Winter X Games. The best snowboarders in the world race in these games.

19

Stay safe. Wear a helmet like this racer. Maybe one day you will be a racer, too. Have fun snowboarding!

Glossary

air to fakie (AYR TO FAY-kee) A special snowboarding move, or trick, where the rider and the board turn in the air.

alpine (AL-pyn) Relating to hills or mountains.

bindings (BYN-dingz) Something used to hold your boots onto the snowboard.

freestyle (FREE-styl) A kind of snowboarding where you go high in the air and do different tricks.

goggles (GOG-elz) A kind of eyeglasses that fit close around your eyes. They are used to protect eyes from light, snow, or dust.

helmet (HEL-mit) What snowboarders wear to keep their heads safe.

racer (RAY-sir) A person who is in a race against another person or other people.

tricks (TRIHKS) Special, or difficult, moves or stunts.

Winter X Games (WIN-ter EKS GAYMS) When extreme sportsmen and sportswomen around the world play against each other to decide who is the best in their sport.

Here are more books to read about snowboarding:

Snowboarding: A Complete Guide for Beginners
by George Sullivan
Puffin (1997)

The Fantastic Book of Snowboarding
by Lesley McKenna and Catherine Wood
Copper Beech Books (1998)

To learn more about snowboarding, check out these Web sites:

http://www.aboutsnowboarding.com
http://www.usaa.org

Index

A
air to fakie, 16
alpine, 12

B
bindings, 10
boots, 10

F
freestyle, 14

G
goggles, 6

H
helmet, 6, 20

R
racer, 20

S
snow, 4

T
tricks, 14, 16, 18

W
Winter X Games, 18

Word Count: 138

Note to Librarians, Teachers, and Parents

If reading is a challenge, Reading Power is a solution! Reading Power is perfect for readers who want high-interest subject matter at an accessible reading level. These fact-filled, photo-illustrated books are designed for readers who want straightforward vocabulary, engaging topics, and a manageable reading experience. With clear picture/text correspondence, leveled Reading Power books put the reader in charge. Now readers have the power to get the information they want and the skills they need in a user-friendly format.